Tsarskoye Selo

Palaces and Parks

2004

Introduction by IVAN SAUTOV
Text by GALINA KHODASEVICH
English translation by PAUL WILLIAMS
Design by VITALY VIAZOVSKY

Photographs by LEONID BOGDANOV, VALERY GORDT, PAVEL IVANOV,
ALEXANDER MININ, YURY MOLOKOVETS, NIKOLAI RAKHMANOV,
VICTOR SAVIK, VLADIMIR SHLIAKAN, YEVGENY SINIAVER,
OLEG TRUBSKY and VITALY VIAZOVSKY

Managing editor NINA GRISHINA
Editor and proof-reader MARIA LYZHENKOVA
Computer typesetter IRINA SEROVA
Colour correction by TATIANA KRAKOVSKAYA and YEKATERINA SHUMIKHINA

Tsarskoye Selo is a unique architectural monument of the eighteenth to early twentieth centuries, including two former grand imperial residences — the Catherine and Alexander Palaces.

In its 300-year history the palace-and-park ensemble has experienced wars and revolutions, trials and tribulations, but has come through everything thanks to the devoted work of the museum staff. Restoring the Catherine Palace demanded decades of painstaking creative labour by restorers who invested no less artistic feeling and talent in the place than the craftsmen of the past. Today we can reckon the work to be near completion. The recreation of the famous Golden Enfilade is finished, the legendary Amber Room shines again in all its glory. The Tsarskoye Selo parks, returned to their historical layout, delight the eye. Restoration work continues in the Alexander Palace too and there is hope that with time the interiors there can be brought back completely. The museum has set itself the difficult task of bringing real life to its historical monuments. This is a goal for such newly-restored pavilions as the Tower Ruin and the White Tower: to enable visitors not only to admire the works of architecture we have recovered, but also to take part in knightly tournaments and other theatricalized events.

We hope that soon we will be able to present the superb suburban ensemble of Tsarskoye Selo to the public in all its splendour.

Ivan Sautov
Director, the Tsarskoye Selo
Museum Preserve

gotiations with foreign ambassadors, "royal conferences" and State Councils.

The area where Tsarskoye Selo would eventually appear belonged in the Middle Ages to the Russian principality of Novgorod. In the fifteenth century the Novgorodian lands, including the southern shore of the Gulf of Finland, became part of the Muscovite state. Later, in the early 17th century, the area was seized by Sweden and it was only a hundred years later, during the Northern War (1700–21), that Russia recovered the Neva and access to the Baltic. The construction of St Petersburg began and simultaneously suburban imperial residences started to appear around the city. On 24 June 1710 Peter the Great issued an order granting Saari-Mois ("the manor on an island") to Catherine Alexeyevna — a woman of humble Livoni-

◀ *Girolamo Bon.* **Portrait of Peter the Great.** *1833*

Ivan Adolsky. **Portrait of Empress Catherine I with a Moorish Boy.** *After 1725*

Tsarskoye Selo occupies a special place among the suburbs of St Petersburg. A refined spot, full of poetic charm, it attracts anyone who has a love of the beautiful. The grand Catherine and Alexander Palaces that gave their names to the surrounding parks, the host of pavilions, sculptures, summer-houses and other features have not only artistic, but also historical significance. The Tsarskoye Selo ensemble is directly associated with major figures in Russia's past: Peter the Great and Catherine I, their daughter Elizabeth, Catherine II, Alexei Orlov, Piotr Rumiantsev, Grigory Potemkin, Alexander I, Nicholas I, Nicholas II and many more. For two centuries this summer residence of the rulers of Russia was the setting for diplomatic receptions, ne-

Friedrich Hartmann Barisien. **View of the Great Palace at Tsarskoye Selo.** *1760*

an origins who in 1712 became Peter's wife and in 1725 Empress in her own right. This gift determined the subsequent fate of the relatively small estate. Between 1716 and 1726 the first masonry residence was constructed here and a regular Dutch-style garden laid out.

The middle years of the eighteenth century were marked by major work to reconstruct the palace that Catherine left after Empress Elizabeth, the favourite daughter of Peter the Great, came into possession of her mother's old estate. The creation of the palace-and-park ensemble was entrusted to such celebrated architects as Mikhail Zemtsov, Andrei Kvasov, Savva Chevakinsky and, finally, Bartolomeo Francesco Rastrelli. On an area of less than 100 acres those masters created a magnificent composition in the spirit of Versailles. Rastrelli directed all the work on the elaborate architec-

tural complex from 1748 onwards and by the end of 1756 the Tsarskoye Selo residence was in the main complete. The Catherine Palace dazzled contemporaries with the brilliant splendour of its Baroque facades. In the main palace building Rastrelli decorated forty state rooms and more than 100 residential and ancillary rooms. Sixteen of the state rooms located on the main floor made up the celebrated Golden Enfilade.

In the park adjoining the eastern side of the palace, magnificent terraces with elaborate flowerbeds, smooth ponds and marble sculpture formed further whimsical Baroque compositions. Ornately trimmed trees turned the alleys into green corridors that led to pavilions intended for balls and grand receptions. Elizabeth loved to entertain in the Hermitage pavilion where, when the dancing was at its height, the floor would suddenly part to make way for tables set with luxurious fare. Rich dishes would appear equally unexpectedly on the tables, delivered there by special lifting mechanisms.

In the Old Garden, as the Catherine Park was originally known, a special role was played by the Great Pond. It was on the shores of this man-made body of water that Rastrelli placed the grandest structures in the park — the Grotto and the Coasting Hill. Elizabeth decided to give the elegant Grotto that looked as light as the foam on waves, the appearance of a sea cave and had the interior decorated with shells.

Elizabeth's unexpected death in 1761 did not put an end to the development of the ensemble. Catherine II, the next mistress of Tsarskoye Selo, confessed that "plantomania" — creating parks — was a real passion with her. She gave orders to change the old regular layout and construct new compositions in the manner of the then-fashionable English landscape parks. The Catherine Park grew in size; the regularly-shaped pond turned into the Great Lake. Sweeping meadows laid out on the slopes of hills provided a setting for isolated (planted) stands of trees. Pavilions in a host of different architectural styles and tastes were constructed in the park. Gothic castles and summerhouses combined with ancient ruins, Classical edifices coexisted with imitation mediaeval and Chinese pavilions. Catherine employed as architects Yury Velten, Antonio Rinaldi, Giacomo

Empress Elizabeth Strolling at Tsarskoye Selo 1905. Watercolour by Yevgeny Lanseray

**The Hermitage in
the Park at Tsarskoye Selo.** *1759*
*After a drawing by Michael Makhaeyev,
engraved by Alexei Grekov*

Quarenghi, Vasily Neyelov and his sons, Ilya and Piotr. Columns and obelisks were also erected to commemorate victories in Russia's wars against Turkey, reminders of triumphs on land and sea that had amazed the whole of Europe.

The Italian Giacomo Quarenghi and the Scot Charles Cameron created a whole complex in the style of the Ancient World. Cameron put up buildings inspired by Roman *thermae*: the Cold Bath and Agate Rooms together with a colonnaded gallery designed as a promenade with fine views. The works of Russian architects rivalled those of their foreign colleagues. An entire dynasty of Neyelovs laboured successfully to turn Catherine's fantasies into reality. Vasily Neyelov and his two sons were responsible the majority of the pavilions.

Fiodor Rokotov. Portrait of Empress
Catherine II. *Late 1770s – 1780s* ▶

The St Petersburg architect Yury Velten also devised unusual features for the park. The year 1786 saw the appearance of the Creaking Summerhouse (1773), stylized in imitation of an old Chinese pavilion, and the Tower Ruin, resembling a mediaeval stronghold. By the end of the eighteenth century more than thirty pieces of architecture had been installed in the extended part of the Catherine Park.

In 1796, in the Alexander Park that had been a continuation of the Old Garden, Giacomo Quarenghi constructed the Alexander Palace. The building was commissioned by Catherine II for her grandson, the future Emperor Alexander I. The new residence did not have the resplendence of the Catherine Palace: its Classical style owed its effect to strict proportions and restrained decor. The main facade of the Alexander Palace is adorned by a majestic Corinthian colonnade. Subsequently the Alexan-

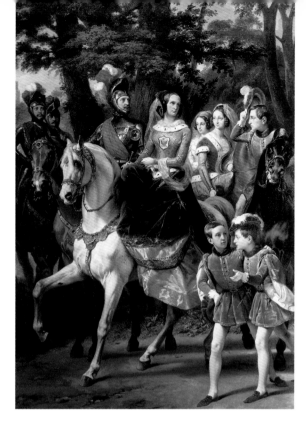

Horace Vernet
The Tsarskoye Selo Carousel. *1843*

French artist Horace Vernet in the painting *Tsarskoye Selo Carousel*. That was the name given to a mounted tournament held to mark Nicholas's silver wedding anniversary in 1842. The participants were provided with authentic knightly armour from the Arsenal.

The palace attained its greatest importance, though, in the reign of Nicholas II. The last ruler of the Romanov dynasty made the Alexander Palace his permanent residence. It is this palace that is associated with the final chapter in the history of the Russian Empire: it was here that the arrested former Emperor was brought from army headquarters in Mogilev, and from here that the whole family was moved to Siberia before being shot in Yekaterinburg.

Ernst Friedrich von Liphart
Portrait of Emperor Nicholas II. *1900*

der Park began to exist and develop separately from the Catherine Park. It consists of the geometrically laid-out Upper (or Old) Garden and landscape compositions by the palace and in the Menagerie area. The landscape area is the more extensive, almost 500 acres, and was formed in place of the Menagerie. Emperor Nicholas I made the Alexander Palace his favourite residence and new architectural features were created in the park: the Arsenal, White Tower and Chapelle.

The architects Adam Menelaws and Piotr Neyelov erected "Gothic" towers and fortifications in the park, giving them the appearance of romantic mediaeval ruins. The Arsenal housed Nicholas I's celebrated collection of historical European arms and armour. Contemporaries called the Emperor the knightly monarch. He was recorded in this guise by the

The children of Nicholas II:
Olga, Tatiana, Maria, Anastasia
and Tsesarevich Alexei
Early 20th-century photograph

◀ *Yegor Meyer.* **The Garden Facade**
of the New (Alexander) Palace. *1840s*

Following the invasion by Nazi Germany in June 1941, the most valuable items of furnishing were evacuated to the rear of the country. On 17 September 1941 the palaces at Tsarskoye Selo were taken by Hitler's forces. There followed plundering of the remaining treasures, destruction of the interior decoration and fires. Nothing was left of the palaces but charred ruins and ravaged halls. Several decades were required to restore the interiors of the Catherine and Alexander Palaces.

In contrast to other imperial residences that have fully "risen from the ashes", the museum in the Alexander Palace is only beginning its post-war history. The public can

Part of a wall of the Amber Room ▶

◀ The Green Dining-Room in the Catherine Palace. Photograph from 1944

visit a display housed in the personal apartments of Nicholas II and Empress Alexandra. In the left wing of the building the decor of the State Study and Nicholas II's Reception Room has survived. There too visitors can see genuine items that belonged to the palace's crowned occupants.

Documents and pictures, archive records and inventories enabled the restorers to recreate the interiors of the Catherine Palace where sumptuous Baroque halls created by Rastrelli combine with the refined interiors of Cameron and the austere studies of Vasily Stasov. Up to now about thirty interiors have been restored. St Petersburg craftsmen spent over three decades recreating the mosaics of the Amber Room that was plundered by the Nazi occupiers during the Second World War. At the same time others reproduced the carved and gilded wall-lights, mosaic allegories of the senses — *Sight, Hearing, Taste,*

Touch and Smell, the parquet floor made of precious varieties of wood and the ceiling painting *The Marriage of Chronos*. The re-creation of the Amber Room was finished for the 300th anniversary of St Petersburg.

The beauty of the Tsarskoye Selo palace interiors, the atmosphere of art and poetry in its old parks has always attracted poets, writers, artists and musicians. The names of many major figures in Russian culture from the first half of the eighteenth century onwards are closely associated with the residence and the town that grew up beside it.

Many poets spent their young years here, including Anna Akhmatova and Nikolai Gumilev. It is, however, most celebrated as the birthplace of the muse of Russia's greatest poet, Alexander Pushkin (1799–1837), who was among the first pupils of the Lyceum, an elite educatinal establishment for sons of the nobility that Emperor Alexander I established in a building alongside the Catherine Palace in 1811. He wrote his first verses here and, in the course of his life, dedicated more than 130 works to Tsarskoye Selo, extolling its park landscapes, architecture and monuments. The poet referred to the town as his home-land. The memory of Pushkin is preserved within the walls of the famous Lyceum, now a museum, and in its garden with the bronze statue of the young Pushkin by Robert Bach installed there in 1900.

The monument to Pushkin in the Lyceum garden. Sculptor: Robert Bach. 1900

АЛЕКСАНДРУ СЕРГѢЕВИЧУ
ПУШКИНУ.

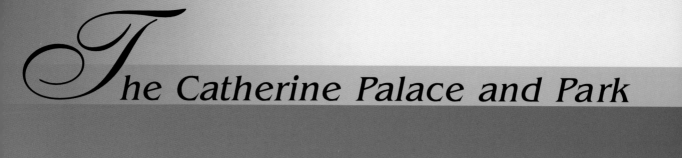

The Catherine Palace and Park

The facade of the Catherine Palace seen from the central alley of the Catherine Park. Architect: Bartolomeo Francesco Rastrelli. 1752–56

The elegant Catherine Palace, set on a tall hill (65 metres above sea level), became the centre of a whole ensemble. With its snow-white columns set off by sky blue walls, abundant gilding and sculpture and a crop of gold domes, it dominates the surrounding space. The palace was the work of famous architects Mikhail Zemtsov, Andrei Kvasov, Savva Chevakinsky and, most significantly, Bartolomeo Francesco Rastrelli, who gave the ensemble its final form. The Catherine Palace astonished contemporaries with its magnificent abundance of architectural decoration. The interiors came to reflect various styles, chiefly Baroque and Classical. Some rooms were reworked in the mid-nineteenth century in keeping with the taste for historicism then prevailing.

At present the museum display comprises twenty-eight restored halls, including the state rooms of the Golden Enfilade created by Rastrelli, the personal apartments of Catherine II's son, the future Paul I, that were redesigned by Charles Cameron, and a few rooms that belonged to Emperor Alexander I and were decorated by Vasily Stasov.

The Church Wing of the Catherine Palace. 1750s, 1860s
Architects: Bartolomeo Francesco Rastrelli, A. Vidov ▶

**Moulded window embrasures
of the Catherine Palace**

The architect's treatment of the 302-metre (almost 1,000 feet) facade puts the palace among the masterpieces of the Russian Baroque. Figures of atlantes alternate with male and female masks. The capitals of the columns and window surrounds are decorated with fanciful moulded compositions created in the mid-eighteenth century from models by the sculptor Johann Duncker. No less opulent is the decoration of the state rooms. The halls used for official receptions were located on the second storey and placed along on a single axis, forming what became known as the Golden Enfilade. The personal apartments of Empress Maria Fiodorovna, wife of Paul I, their son Grand Duke Alexander (Alexander I) and his brother Konstantin formed another suite known as the Small Enfilade. The decoration of many rooms was destroyed during the Second World War and restoration work is still going on.

**Pilaster console on the facade
of the Catherine Palace**

◀ **Atlantes on the facade
of the Catherine Palace. 1750s
Architect: Bartolomeo Francesco Rastrelli;
sculptor: Johann Franz Duncker**

The clock on the Main Staircase of the Catherine Palace

A visit inside the palace begins with the Grand Staircase. Before the reconstruction undertaken by Catherine II, the main staircase was located in the south wing, while the centre of the building here was occupied by a splendid Chinese Hall. In 1780 Charles Cameron replaced it with a mahogany staircase. In 1860 the interior was reworked by Ippolito Monighetti who adorned the walls and ceilings with Rococo-style ornament reminiscent of Rastrelli's interiors. The carved white marble balustrade was complemented by moulded scrolls, volutes and garlands painted white. The walls also bear a clock and barometer as well as Chinese and Japanese porcelain placed on white decorative consoles. Like the majority of the palace interiors the Grand Staircase was badly damaged during the war. It was restored in the 1960s. The unique collection of Oriental ceramics was among the items saved by evacuation beyond the Urals.

Beyond the Grand Staircase lay the apartments making up the Golden Enfilade. Foremost among them is the Great Hall. In the eighteenth century it was known as the "Bright Gallery" on account of its elongated shape and the host of glazed doors and windows. The hall is impressive for its immense size (831,5 square metres) and elaborate decorative compositions.

The Main Staircase. 1860. Architect: Ippolito Monighetti ▶

The Great Hall. 1750s. Architect: Bartolomeo Francesco Rastrelli

The dominant decorative element in the Great Hall is the gilded carving. One hundred and thirty Russian craftsmen worked from Rastrelli's designs and Duncker's models to produce the woodwork for the hall. Under their skilled hands, limewood came to life, turning into lively cupids among the upper tiers of windows or exquisite female figures — the caryatids so typical of the Baroque style. The ceiling painting on the subject of *The Triumph of Russia* was created in 1753 from a sketch by the noted Italian decorative painter Giuseppe Valeriani. Its three allegorical elements fill the entire surface of an enormous ceiling. Mirrors, a patterned parquet floor and gilded wooden chairs added to the architectural impression.

◀ *The Great Hall. Detail of the gilded wood-carving. 1750s*

The Third Antechamber. Ceiling painting:
Mount Olympus. 1750s; 1980s
Artist: Pietro Gradizzi

The Great Hall was the setting for gala dinners, great masked balls and assemblies. It was said that "there seem not to have been any crowned heads who have visited Tsarskoye Selo and not sat down to a banquet in this hall." (In Nicholas II's reign it was used for meals on days when the Emperor reviewed his troops, as well as for family celebrations.) Court life in the eighteenth century was an endless round of festivities. In March 1757 the British ambassador wrote that since the previous Wednesday there had been no less than three masked balls and one opera, and not a single day in the week had gone by without some sort of amusement.

Glazed doors lead from the Great Hall to three Antechambers with rich gilded decoration. These were intended for formal receptions and served in the evenings for gatherings, concerts, theatrical performances and "chamber balls".

◄ **The Third Antechamber**
in the Great Palace at Tsarskoye Selo
1865. Watercolour by A.H. Kolb

22

The Third Antechamber. Detail of the decoration

Formal banquets and suppers of various kinds occupied a significant place in eighteenth-century court life. The tables were set with immense silver vessels, pyramids of confectionery, decorations made of porcelain and sugar that was then imported from distant lands. Fountains pouring out wine, coloured water and champagne were usually installed in the centre of the tables. Nowadays the appearance of such "festive boards" has been recreated in several rooms of the palace.

The Cavalier's Dining-Room was used more often than other halls for receptions involv-

◀ *The Cavaliers' Dining-Room*
Boule-de-neige vase (scent-holder)
19th century. Meissen, Germany. Porcelain

The Cavaliers' Dining-Room
The Order Service. Basket and sugar-
bowl. 1780s. Gardner Factory,
Russia. Porcelain

The Cavaliers' Dining-Room. 1750s. Architect: Bartolomeo Francesco Rastrelli

ing small numbers of people. On display here are items from the four "Order services" produced at the private Gardner porcelain factory outside Moscow in the 1780s. The name derives from the fact that the items in the services were decorated with the ribbons and other insignia of Russian military orders of chivalry founded in the eighteenth century: St Andrew the First-Called, St George the Bringer of Victory, St Alexander Nevsky and the Sainted Prince Vladimir. Large formal serv-

ices, in the sense of sets of tableware with different functions, made in the same material and sharing elements of decoration, first appeared in Russia in the reign of Empress Elizabeth. As well as porcelain services the table would be set with glass drinking vessels. Wine was served in bottles, occasionally in carafes (*shtofy*). Various items made from porcelain were used to decorate the halls. Vases were often placed on small tables in front of mirrors for greater effect.

The White State Dining-Room. 1750s. Architect: Bartolomeo Francesco Rastrelli

The White State Dining-Room was intended for ordinary court dinners. The table was usually laid for the imperial family here when there were no visiting guests. In the absence of the Empress, the court dined in the White State Dining-Room. Today the room presents an appearance typical of the eighteenth century. A "must" for such ceremonial dinners were the elaborately shaped tables also designed by the architect Rastrelli. Great attention was paid to the way in which the tables were decorated. In eighteenth-century sources we can read such details as: "For banquets the tablecloths are to be artfully hung with scarlet and green ribbons and fastened with pins, while the tables are to be decorated with figures." Elaborate dining ceremonial

was matched by refined table settings. The table now displays a porcelain service with "Indian flowers" made at Meissen in Germany in the 1730s.The furniture here consists of carved and gilded console tables and chairs that were made in imitation of surviving originals.

In the mid-eighteenth century European tastes in art spread to Russia and paintings became a typical adornment of palace halls.

A palace dining room would invariably contain a type of china cabinet that rationally combined a chest of drawers and a display-case. The examples in this room were made in Germany and the Netherlands in the early eighteenth century. They are decorated with a range of plant ornament and filled with porcelain produced at

The White State Dining-Room
Johann Friedrich Grooth
Dead Game. 1740s

Canvases by the court artist Johann Grooth, who worked in Russia for 58 years, adorn the walls of the White State Dining-Room. These paintings were part of a series of forty-six that Grooth produced to decorate the Monbijou hunting pavilion in the Tsarskoye Selo garden. Later some of the works, depicting hunting trophies, were moved to the palace itself. Grooth's work was something entirely new in Russian artistic life and played a major role in the evolution of the "hunting still life". The paintings in this room include Dead Game, Storks *and* White Peacocks.

The White State
Dining-Room. Buffet-secretaire
18th century. Germany

Meissen and at the St Petersburg Imperial Factory. The walls are lined in carved and gilded frames with white cloth featuring a large flower pattern that was hand-woven in the 1970s on the basis of an eighteenth-century sample. The decoration of the hall is completed by a ceiling painting — *The Triumph of Apollo*, a nineteenth-century copy of a well known work by the Italian Guido Reni. Apollo, one of the chief figures of Classical mythology, leader of the muses and also identified with the god of sunlight Helios. This method of decorating the ceilings in the halls of the enfilade in the Catherine Palace dates back to the middle of the nineteenth century. Today those canvases that were lost during the war years have been replaced in the majority of the halls by the works of other artists, mainly of the Italian school, on subjects from ancient mythology.

The large festive gatherings held in the Great Hall and in the Antechambers ended with celebrations for a select group of the guests held in the rooms of the enfilade. In order to make each room unique, Rastrelli used a variety of artistic devices. In the Crimson and Green Pilaster Rooms he divided the walls with glazed pilasters. Coloured foil was placed behind the glass, creating an effect like precious stones glistening in elaborate gilded frames. The red and green pilasters look especially striking set off by the white cloth-lined walls.

In the eighteenth century these rooms had no definite functional purpose. The Crimson Pilaster Room was used as a games room. In the centre is a card-table used to display a unique carved ivory chess-set made in China in the eighteenth century. It has a board inlaid with splendid pieces of mother-of-pearl. The visitor's attention is drawn to a bureau inlaid with various varieties of wood. It was produced by the German master craftsman Abraham Roentgen. This item is not only a splendid example of the cabinet maker's art in its time, but also a complex piece of construction with concealed secret drawers. It was purchased in Germany on the orders of Catherine II. The collection of furniture

The Crimson Pilaster Room. 1750s. Architect: Bartolomeo Francesco Rastrelli

The Crimson Pilaster Room. Painted tiles on the stove

is completed by several more card-tables. The ceiling is decorated with a painting entitled *The Mercy of Alexander the Great* by an unknown seventeenth-century artist. The subject is the triumph and magnanimity of the great general who frees the captured Persian king Darius and his family.

The restored tiled heating stove differs from others that can be found adorning the palace interiors. It has an elaborate architectural form with a variety of niches, arches and columns made from special plaster elements imitating the old tiles. The tiles bear depictions of typical members of different European social groups in national costume. This exceptionally wide range of decorative painting was reproduced after the war by R.D. Slepushkina from surviving photographs as the majority of tiled stoves in the palace were destroyed in the war. The work was carried out by hand on the plaster panels that substituted for the old tiles. The shine and barely noticeable yellowing that makes the plaster look like tiles comes from a special synthetic coating.

Especially splendid in the Crimson Pilaster Room are the *dessus-de-portes* — the carved panels over the doors that are made up of rocailles with garlands and baskets of flowers.

The Green Pilaster Room. 1750s. Architect: Bartolomeo Francesco Rastrelli

The Green Pilaster Room produces a monumental impression. Here Rastrelli the interior decorator demonstrates his talents once again. He used two tiers of windows to change the perceived height and width of the walls. The glazed pilasters seem to recede into the depths of the room glistening with a mysterious green gleam. In the corner is an elegant stove decorated with "Hamburg tiles" (recreated) a standard element in all Rastrelli's interiors. In his time there were 79 tiled stoves in the palace. A separate inventory made in 1753 reveals that the state rooms alone contained more than forty of them.

A major role in the decoration of the Green Pilaster Room is played by mirrors and paintings. The centre of the ceiling is filled with a canvas painted by V. Lednev in the 1970s that reproduces a ceiling painting by the eighteenth-century Italian artist Stefano Torelli, *A Resting Warrior Heeds Summons of the Muses*. The god of war Mars is depicted surrounded by the nine muses. In Catherine II's time the room served as a butler's pantry and was separated by a thin partition in the Neo-Gothic style. Nowadays the furniture consists of a sofa and chairs that were manufactured in France in the early nineteenth century. The walnut bureau is the work of an unknown eighteenth-century German craftsman. It was used for keeping precious jewellery as well as letters and documents.

◀ *The Golden Enfilade. 1750s. Architect: Bartolomeo Francesco Rastrelli*

Ivan Adolsky. **Portrait of Empress Catherine I with a Moorish Boy.** *After 1725*

Portraits of emperors and empresses of the Romanov dynasty occupy a large place in the palace's collection of paintings. The Portrait Hall contains a celebrated portrait of Catherine I painted about 1725 by the Russian artist Ivan Adolsky. The Empress is depicted in a formal gown with the sash of the Order of St Andrew the First-Called and attributes of imperial power. Catherine was far from a beauty, "yet there is in the full cheeks, the upturned nose, the velvety eyes, at one moment languorous, at another ardent, in her scarlet lips and round chin, indeed in her whole physiognomy so much torrid passion … that it is not hard to grasp why such a colossus as Peter gave himself up en-tirely to this 'friend of the heart'." The same hall also contains a portrait of Catherine's daughter, Empress Elizabeth, painted posthu-mously by the German artist Heinrich Buchholtz in the 1760s. As befits a gala portrait, the art-ist created an idealized, abstracted image of the Empress. The details of her costume — ac-cessories, rich fabrics, ermine — are painted with great skill, producing an appropriate sense of imposing formality. On the wall opposite the windows are portraits of Peter the Great's sis-ter Natalia and Catherine II. The former is a copy of a work by the Russian eighteenth-cen-tury artist Ivan Nikitin, the latter a copy of a portrait by Fiodor Rokotov.

The Portrait Hall. 1750s. Architect: Bartolomeo Francesco Rastrelli

Probably the most famous room in the Golden Enfilade created by Rastrelli in the 1750s is the Amber Room — a unique interior with decoration that incorporated mosaic panels made up of pieces of amber of different size and colour.

The majority of these mosaics were presented to Peter the Great in 1716 by King Frederick William I of Prussia. In 1755 Empress Elizabeth had the panels moved to Tsarskoye Selo, where Rastrelli skilfully fitted them into the palace, installing them between mirror pilasters, adding gilded carved ornament and a painted frieze. He also added four

Florentine mosaics forming a series allegorically depicting the senses in splendid carved frames. This unique room adorned the Catherine Palace for almost two centuries. The amber panels were plundered by the Nazis, taken to Königsberg in East Prussia in 1942, and disappeared without trace in 1945. Since then the fate of this masterpiece has remained a mystery. There are many versions of what became of the Amber Room, but none has yet been proved true. In July 1979 the government of the Russian Federation decided to have the amber panels recreated and in 1983 work began following a project de

◀◀ *The Amber Room. 1750s. Architect: Bartolomeo Francesco Rastrelli*

◀ *The Amber Room. Detail of a panel with an amber frame containing the Florentine mosaic* Sight

The Amber Room. Detail of a panel containing the monogram of Frederick I of Prussia

vised by the architect A. Kedrinsky. The panels have now been recreated by St Petersburg craftsmen with the financial support of the German company *Ruhrgas AG* that has been importing Russian natural gas since 1973.

The end of this painstaking process has been timed to coincide with the 300th anniversary of St Petersburg as a sort of present to the city on that occasion. Some 5.7 tonnes of raw amber, including wastage, was used to bring back the Amber Room. At the same time as the panels, restorers from the *Tsarskoye Selo Amber Workshop* company have completed the recreation of the four Florentine mosaics. One original mosaic, an allegory of touch and smell, was discovered in Germany after the war and returned to Russia by the German government. Gilded decoration on the walls and mirror pilasters have been created as in the eighteenth century, and a parquet floor produced from precious varieties of wood. Using a sketch by an unknown eighteenth-century artist of the Italian school now in the Hermitage, Ya. Kazakov and B. Lebedev have produced a ceiling painting entitled *The Marriage of Chronos*.

The Amber Room. Calendar clock in the form of a tree and pastoral scene. Circa 1750. Paris ▶

The Picture Hall. 1750s. Architect: Bartolomeo Francesco Rastrelli

The Picture Hall, another of Rastrelli's creations, displays a unique artistic approach. In the eighteenth century this hall was also used for banquets and known therefore as the Picture Dining-Room. It was also the setting for diplomatic receptions. The hall harmoniously combines paintings, brightly gilded door surrounds, cobalt-painted tiled stoves and colourful parquet floors. The elegant pattern of the parquet, formed from precious varieties of wood, the symmetrically placed heating stoves and the ceiling painting depicting the gods on Olympus in combination with opulent carved woodwork make this one of the grandest rooms in the palace. The coving, decorated with garlands of flowers and figured compositions, serves as a sort of frame, a neat transition from the paintings on the wall to the image on the ceiling. The ceiling painting, recreated in the post-war years, is a copy of the one by the eighteenth-century artist Gasparo Diziani above the Jordan Staircase of the Winter Palace in St Petersburg. The tall mirrors between the windows are complemented by decorative painted panels and set in opulent carved and gilded frames. The symmetrically placed doors are flanked by caryatids, while in the centre of the compositions above is Minerva, the goddess of wisdom, patroness of science and crafts, resting on a mirror supplied by a winged Cupid.

Still, the chief treasure here is the collection of works by outstanding Western European artists of the seventeenth and early eighteenth centuries: landscapes, battle pieces, genre scenes, still lifes, historical and mythological compositions.

The core of the display in the Picture Hall was a collection from Prague acquired for the palace in 1745 by the artist Georg Grooth on Elizabeth's orders. One hundred and thirty works by representatives of different European schools adorn the north and south walls. In pursuit of an overall decorative effect Rastrelli employed the "tapestry" method of hanging paintings, taking into account neither the subjects of the paintings nor their artistic worth, but only their ca-

pacity to produce a certain impression of colour. This method, implemented by the artist Lucas Pfandzelt, provided a new way of using paintings in an interior. When the Picture Hall was created the collection was supplemented with works brought from Peterhof and others bought in Germany. The paintings have now hung in the hall for almost 250 years. In 1941 museum staff managed to evacuate the majority of them. Replacements for the missing sixteen were selected from the stocks of Leningrad museums after the war.

Noteworthy among the works are Dutch and Flemish landscapes by Jan Both and realistic

Clock with the allegorical composition Peace and Abundance. 1770. Paris, France
Sculptor: Jean-Louis Prieur; clock mechanism by A. Peltier; from a design by François Boucher

genre scenes by Adriaen van Ostade and David Teniers. A bold decorative quality marks both the architectural compositions of Emanuel de Witte and the still lifes of Jan Fyt. Among the French and Italian works mention should be made of the allegories of sculpture and music by Jean Nattier, the battle scenes of Jacques Courtois (Bourgignon), as well as mythological and biblical scenes by Jean Blanchard, Luca Giordano, Antonio Balestra and others. A special place belongs to two works painted by the Frenchman Pierre Denis Martin the Younger — *The Battle of Poltava* and *The Battle of Perevolochnia*. They were commissioned by Peter the Great who was concerned to preserve the memory of Russia's glorious victories in the Northern War (1700–21). The pair were moved here from Peterhof on the personal instructions of Empress Elizabeth, who had them placed in this room in remembrance of her father.

The Picture Hall reveals Russia's historical and cultural ties with Europe.

Jean-Marc Nattier. An Allegory of Music
First half of the 18th century

Jan Both. Spanish Landscape. *First half of the 17th century*

The Drawing-Room of Alexander I. 1750s, 1820s
Architects: Bartolomeo Francesco Rastrelli, Vasily Stasov

The rooms beyond the Picture Hall were a continuation of Rastrelli's enfilade. They retain their typical mid-eighteenth-century decoration. The walls of Alexander I's Drawing-Room bear paintings of the imperial family by the noted court artist Louis Caravaque. There are four of his works here, portraits of Catherine I, Peter the Great, Elizabeth and Anna Ivanovna. The portrait of Catherine II is a contemporary copy of a work by Johann-Baptist Lampi (the Elder), while the large full-length portrait of Alexander I is by George Dawe. The ceiling painting, *Venus in a Chariot*, is a copy of a work by Boucher.

Louis Caravaque. Portrait of Empress
Anna Ivanovna. 1730s

The Drawing-Room of Alexander I. Ceiling painting: Venus in a Chariot
Copy from a painting by François Boucher

The Green Dining-Room. 1780s. Architect: Charles Cameron

In the 1770s, the "Minerva of Tsarskoye Selo", as contemporaries called Catherine II, decided to alter the decor in some of the rooms. She entrusted the work to the Scot Charles Cameron who came to Russia in 1779. He used a strict Classical style in his designs for Catherine's personal rooms in the south of the palace and the apartments of her heir, Grand Duke Paul, and his wife Maria Fiodorovna in the north.

The interiors of the Green Dining-Room, the Blue State Drawing-Room and the Bedchamber reflect the vogue for the Ancient World. The walls of the Green Dining-Room are decorated with white sculptural figures, rectangular reliefs and round medallions. Their pale pink background adds to the soft, bright colour scheme of the interior. The sculptural elements of the decoration — figures of naked youths and girls in ancient clothing — were splendidly executed by Ivan Martos who managed to invest forms with particular harmony and expressiveness. The design of the doors is complemented by arabesque paintings in darker shades of the same set of colours. In the centre of the north wall is a white marble fireplace flanked by lion-mask consoles with carved ornament. It has a gilded bronze fireguard and andirons in the shape of sphinxes. The fire-irons were produced to Cameron's designs.

The Green Dining-Room. The fireplace ▶

The Blue State Drawing-Room of Grand Duke Paul and Grand Duchess Maria Fiodorovna, the largest and most elegant room in the northern apartments, received a host of unexpected famous guests. We cannot tell whether the departed souls of the former occupants return to the restored halls, but still today their faces look sternly down on visitors here from the old portraits depicting Paul and Maria Fiodorovna, Peter the Great and Catherine I, Elizabeth and Catherine II.

The creative fantasy of Cameron and the skills of the craftsmen turned every detail into an enchanting work of art. This room, whose three windows overlook the grand courtyard, was used for listened to music, conversation and receiving guests. The walls are lined with silvery silk printed in a flower pattern (produced by the *Red Rose* textile group in Moscow from an old sample). The room contains a pair of marble fireplaces that incorporate elements of the Classical architectural order: exquisite caryatids support the cornice that forms the mantelpiece, while the friezes contain bas-reliefs on mythological subjects. The painting on the ceiling, destroyed in a fire in 1820 and recreated in 1959 from Cameron's design that is kept in the Hermitage, repeats motifs from Ancient Roman art. Of the eighty painted medallions in the frieze only sixteen

The Blue State Drawing-Room. 1780s
Architect: Charles Cameron

Germany who deposed her husband Peter III (Peter the Great's grandson) in 1762 — was painted in 1777 by Fiodor Rokotov and Alexander Roslin. Here too is a likeness of Catherine's son, the future Paul I, in his youth. It was produced by the Swede Alexander Roslin who spent three years (1775–77) in St Petersburg. The portrait of Maria Fiodorovna, is a nineteenth-century copy of a work by Elisabeth Vigée-Lebrun. Love of art coupled with exquisite taste marked the owners of this part of the palace. The relationship between Catherine II and her son was marred by dislike and distrust, but this was one thing they had in common.

◀ *Alexander Roslin.* **Portrait of Grand Duke Paul.** *1777*

Unknown Russian artist
Portrait of Grand Duchess Maria Fiodorovna
Copy of the portrait by Elisabeth Vigée-Lebrun. 19th century

survived; following the restoration they were placed in the wall opposite the windows. The room has retained its old parquet made of rosewood, ebony, palisander, amaranth and other precious woods engraved with geometric ornament. The carved and gilded furniture, bronze fireguard and andirons were all produced in St Petersburg in the eighteenth century to Cameron's designs. The blue glass torcheres were created at the St Petersburg Glassworks in 1792.

The formal portraits that decorate the room are the most interesting in the whole palace collection. The artist Ivan Nikitin made the portrait of Peter the Great in 1715. In 1758 the Dane Vigilius Erichsen painted his daughter, Empress Elizabeth. The portrait of Catherine II — the one-time Princess Sophie Friederike Auguste of Anhalt-Zerbst in

The Chinese Blue Drawing-Room. 1780s. Architect: Charles Cameron

The originality of the Blue Chinese Drawing-Room lies in the successful combination of Classical-style decor with "Chinese" works of decorative art. The oriental motifs enliven the austere Classical look of the interior and give it an exotic character. The walls are lined with silk bearing vivid stylized scenes from "Chinese" life, enclosed in gilded frames . Of particular interest are the white marble fireplaces combined with mirrors in carved and gilded frames. Cameron was the first to use this typically English arrangement in Russia. On the mantelpiece and small table there are porcelain vases made in China and Japan in the seventeenth and eighteenth centuries. A gilded stucco frieze, ceiling painting featuring characters from Classical mythology and decorative painting on the doors add to

the splendour. A unique delight in this room is the patterned parquet floor, with an eight-pointed star in its centre made of mahogany, ebony and rosewood.

During the Second World War the Nazi occupiers plundered the silk from the walls here. The extremely difficult task of restoration was performed by one woman, R.D. Slepushkina, who reproduced all the "Chinese" silk. Guided by a surviving fragment discovered above a fireplace and pre-war photographs, she painted anew the whimsical mountains, clouds and trees, landscapes with fancy bridges, towers and human figures, having developed her own technique for using tempera paints on fabric that completely accorded with the manner and colour scheme of the original.

The name of the Choir Anteroom reflects its location next to the choir gallery of the palace church. The room lacks a strong sense of style as it has been redecorated several times. Cameron created two rooms here, one pink, the other straw-coloured. In the 1840s Stasov joined them into one and decorated it with wallpaper. Later the moulded frieze was added and the decorative painting on the ceiling. The walls were once lined with Chinese silk, but since 1894 they have been adorned by silk of a gold colour with a woven pattern featuring pheasants and swans. The bright attractiveness of the present wall covering turns a relatively

The Choir Anteroom ▶
Detail of the wall fabric. 1840s

The Choir Anteroom. 1780s, 1840s. Architects: Charles Cameron, Vasily Stasov

small and modestly finished room into an elegant hall. The silk has an unusual history. The colourful design was created by the French artist Philippe de la Salle for the Lyons factory. From that design the fabric was hand-woven in the late 1770s at the factory belonging to Ivan Lazarev in the village of Frianovo near Moscow. Later, in the nineteenth century, using the same patterns the production of a similar fabric was organized at the Sapozhnikovs' factory outside Moscow. The machine-made fabric was used to upholster the set of grand gilded furniture — a couch and chairs — produced in the eighteenth century to designs

by Rastrelli and also for the curtains in the Choir Anteroom. The unique hand-made eighteenth-century silk was used on the walls. Inlaid tables complete the interior.

On the walls here are two portraits, of Empresses Elizabeth and Catherine II, and a painting of Elizabeth's coronation in the Dormition Cathedral in Moscow.

The Palace Church of the Resurrection itself, designed by Rastrelli, but substantially altered by Stasov after the fire of 1820, is not open to visitors. It was barbarously ruined during the war and has now been conserved rather than restored.

◀ *The Choir Anteroom. Couch. 1750s*
Architect: Bartolomeo Francesco Rastrelli

The Bed-Chamber of Grand Duke Paul. 1780s. Architect: Charles Cameron

The Bedchamber with its delicate faience columns that seem to have come off the walls of some ancient Pompeian building puts one in mind of a Roman temple. It belongs to the "Small Enfilade" — a suite of rooms that was the private preserve of the imperial family. A lady-in-waiting was permanently on duty next to these apartments.

The doors of these private apartments are splendid works of art painted with the figures of fantastic animals and figurative circular, oval and rectangular insets. Moulded medallions on the walls represent in allegorical form happiness, plenty and prosperity. The fine ceramic columns give the room a special charm. They divide up the space, forming an alcove in which the bed stood beneath white silk drapes. Here, as elsewhere, Cameron has made a highlight of an exquisite fireplace combined with a mirror in a carved and gilded frame. The fireplace is decorated with figures of a sleeping Venus and cupids. The little cupids hold vases filled with fruit and flowers. The celebrated craftsmen of Tula (a town with a long history of metal-working and the manufacture of weapons that is located south of Moscow) produced the fireguard of blued steel and gilded bronze and also a little wrought steel table.

The Bed-Chamber of Grand Duke Paul. Fireplace ▶

**The Sculpture (Music) Study. 1780s, 1820
Architects: Charles Cameron, Vasily Stasov**

Adjoining the Bedchamber are two rooms known as the personal apartments of Maria Fiodorovna, the wife of Paul I — the Straw-Coloured Divan Room (or Painting Study) and the Sculpture (or Music) Study. They were intended for Maria Fiodorovna's artistic activities — painting and ivory-carving. Created by Cameron in the 1780s, they were redesigned by Stasov after the fire of 1820.

The golden-yellow hue of the Painting Study, gilded stucco framing the frieze, the cornice and the treatment of the doors have survived from the late eighteenth century. The cross vault, lunettes and frieze were painted anew to Stasov's designs by Dmitry Antonelli following the fire. The maple furniture was created in the nineteenth century in the workshop of Andrei Tour and painted by Giuseppe Bernasconi. On the table there is a French nineteenth-

◀ *The Painting (Straw-Coloured)
Study. 1780s, 1820. Architects:
Charles Cameron, Vasily Stasov*

century bronze and mother-of-pearl "miracle candelabrum".

In the Sculpture Study. The greenish walls are adorned with white bas-reliefs of a Classical character the vaulted ceiling is painted in the monochrome grisaille technique. The fillets of the doors are filled with a white carved ornamental composition with painted insets resembling cameos. On the mahogany desk there is a gilded bronze candelabrum produced in St Petersburg in 1783 to a design by Cameron. The amaranth armchair and the gilded bronze chandelier with faceted crystal were created early in the next century.

Later these rooms housed the private library of Alexander I's wife and also a harp.

◀ *The Sculpture (Music) Study
Detail of the doors*

In the 1820s Vasily Stasov created some new interiors for Alexander I in the Late Classical style. These included the celebrated Marble State Study. Alexander preferred to stay in these rooms, despite the fact that in the final year of her life Catherine II had had the Alexander Palace built for him.

It was in the Catherine Palace that he spent the best and happiest times of his life. In these rooms he found rest and quiet in his later years. The struggle against Napoleon and the complexities of European politics took a considerable spiritual toll on the Liberator of

The Marble (State) Study of Alexander I
The Julius Caesar clock. Before 1817
Workshop of L.F. Feuchere. Chased,
gilded and patinated bronze
with enamel, malachite and marble

◀ *The Marble (State) Study of Alexander I*
Vase bearing a depiction of the entry
of Russian forces into Paris in 1814
19th century. Artist: Jacques François
Joseph Swebach. Imperial Porcelain Factory,
St Petersburg. Gilded and painted porcelain

Europe. The Emperor's personal belongings were kept in the Marble State Study as a memorial following his death in Taganrog.

The austere grandeur of Alexander I's favourite study is emphasized by the unusual finishing of the walls and ceiling — painted in the grisaille technique with ornament consisting mainly of items of ancient arms and armour, a reminder of the victories of 1812–14.

The entrance to the study takes the form of a deep niche separated from the rest of the space by two greenish Ionic columns. Two more columns flank the marble fireplace in the centre of the opposite wall. The lunettes beneath the vault contain scenes from the Greek myth of Cupid and Psyche.

The Persian walnut furniture was produced

to Stasov's designs by the noted St Petersburg craftsmen Grosse and Gambs. The furniture is complemented by a vase made at the Imperial Porcelain Factory in St Petersburg that is decorated with a depiction of Alexander entering Paris in 1814 and a French mantel clock incorporating a figure of the great Roman general Julius Caesar. The Emperor's desk is adorned by a malachite desk set — paperweight, candelabra and writing paraphernalia — from the first quarter of the nineteenth century that was used by Alexander I.

Every item here is suffused with pride in the Russian victory over Napoleon. Incidentally, ideas of the glory and might of Russia are present in each of the celebrated interiors of the Catherine Palace.

The immense restoration work carried out by artists and skilled craftspeople with many different specialities in the Catherine Palace over the almost sixty years since Tsarskoye Selo was liberated has made it possible to restore to life the interiors destroyed during the Nazi occupation. In nearly every room visitors can see photographs showing the state in which the Soviet forces found it on their return. The reborn halls in the palace, like the restored features of the park, carry a charge of exceptional creative energy.

The Marble (State) Study of Alexander I
1820s. Architect: Vasily Stasov

Pierre Lemaire. Architectural Landscape. *17th century*

The Stasov (White) Staircase
1843. Architect: Vasily Stasov ▶

he Catherine Park is interesting for the variety of artistic styles reflected in its layout and in the architecture of its pavilions. A stroll around the park is in many ways a trip into the long history of art in Russia.

The oldest, regular, part of the park is situated in front of the eastern facade of the Catherine Palace. The palace was created as a summer residence and so the opulent festivities, balls and masquerades held there often "spilled over" into the park as a sort of extension to the building. In its alleys and by the main entrances to the palace guests found marble statues and busts of the gods and heroes of Classical mythology.

Sculpture Andromeda. 18th century
Sculptor: Pietro Baratta

◀ *Sculpture Martial Valour. 18th century*
Sculptor: Antonio Tarsia

In the middle of the eighteenth century Empress Elizabeth had over sixty statues brought to Tsarskoye Selo from the Summer Gardens in St Petersburg. A fair number of these were mythological or allegorical works by Italian sculptors. Such pieces as *Glory*, *Love of One's Country* and *Peace* gave attractive physical form to lofty patriotic feelings. Two statues, created by Antonio Tarsia, *Hercules* and *Martial Valour* that flank the Hermitage Alley, are remarkable for their exceptional mastery. A pair of works by the Venetian Pietro Baratta — *Galatea*, a graceful young woman seated on a dolphin, and *Amphitrite*, wife of the sea-god Poseidon — fit naturally into the regular park.

Sculpture Amphitrite. 18th century
Sculptor: Pietro Baratta ▶

◀◀ *The Catherine Park*

The Upper Bath pavilion. 1778. Architect: Ilya Neyelov

The park is situated on flat terraces linked by flights of stone steps. The palace stands on the highest terrace. The second contains parterres with a fanciful pattern worked in coloured sand, coal and greenery placed near the palace so that they could be viewed to good effect from its upper windows; the third a winding maze of alleys. Below again are man-made ponds framed by green lawns.

The recreation of the regular park in its historical form was begun in 1962 to plans drawn up by the prominent architect A.A. Kedrinsky and the landscape gardener N.E. Tumanova and completed in 1978.

At the same time work started on restoring the pavilions that adorn the park.

The Upper Bathhouse stands close to the palace on the bank of one of the mirror ponds. This pavilion was built in 1778 to the design of Ilya Neyelov.

Originally it served as a bathing place for members of the imperial family. The rooms inside are decorated with motifs taken from Nero's Golden House in Ancient Rome.

The facades have been worked in strict Classical style. Pale yellow walls, almost devoid of decoration, accord well with the surrounding formal park.

◄ *Sculptures* **Amphitrite** *and* **Galatea**. *18th century. Sculptor: Pietro Baratta*

A key element in the formation of the architectural character of the park was the elegantly refined pavilions created by Rastrelli. These products of his fanciful imagination, rising above the green hedges, made a single ensemble inseparably linked to the palace. Foremost among them is the Hermitage pavilion, situated in the "Wild Grove", beyond the Fish Canal. The Hermitage was built in 1743–56 to the designs of Mikhail Zemtsov, Savva Chevakinsky and Rastrelli.

The pavilion resembled the palace in colour, architecture and decoration. All the moulded elements on the facade, carved statues and garlands descending from the dome glistened with gold. The area around the pavilion was laid chequer-board-fashion with

Vigilius Erichsen. **Portrait of Empress Elizabeth.** *1758*

The Hermitage Kitchen. 1776. Architect: Vasily Neyelov

black and white marble flags and finished with a balustrade. Both the pavilion itself and the balustrade were adorned with gilded statues and vases.

The upper floor of the Hermitage was occupied by a large formal dining-room finished in the Baroque style: the walls of the hall and four cabinets were decorated with gilded carving, paintings and mirrors. This was a setting for balls and masquerades as well as banquets for foreign ambassadors and ministers. Special lift mechanisms could raise the ready-laid tables, making it possible to do without servants.

The Hermitage Kitchen was constructed nearby, on the bank of the Cascade Canal, in 1776. It was designed by Vasily Neyelov in the "Gothic" style and a granite bridge was built at the same time. The kitchen was used to prepare food for meals in the Hermitage. The idea of creating the canal and bridge came from the engineer Gerard.

◀ *The Hermitage pavilion. 1743–56. Architects: Mikhail Zemtsov, Savva Chevakinsky, Bartolomeo Francesco Rastrelli*

*The **To my dear comrades** Gate. 1818, 1821*
Architects: Vasily Stasov, Adam Menelaws

Gerard designed the eleven weirs, decorated with tufa arches that embellish the Cascade Canal separating the park from the town. The canal was fed from the two Lower Ponds over weirs "scattered" decoratively with rough chunks of natural rock from which the water pours noisily. The Green and Devil's Bridges with their numerous waterfalls reproduced in miniature some romantic wild corners of Scotland.

Russia's victories over Turkey in Catherine II's reign were commemorated in 1771 by the erection of the Morea, or Small Rostral Column between the Lower Ponds. The Roman Doric column is made of blue Olonets marble with white veins and decorated with stylized prows of ships. It was a Roman tradition to erect such columns to mark naval successes. The Triumphal Gate erected nearby in 1817 celebrates the victory over Napoleon.

This edifice, monumental in spite of its relatively small size, takes the form of an austere Doric colonnade. It bears an inscription devised by Alexander I: "To my dear comrades". Either side of the gate the architect Adam Menelaws erected railings decorated by an alternation of ancient shields and military trophies.

The Cascade Bridge. 1777. Engineer: I. Gerard ▶

The Cameron Gallery. 1783–87. Architect: Charles Cameron

On the shore of the Great Lake is the Grotto pavilion, built by Rastrelli in the 1750s. Its facades are embellished with moulded compositions in the form of fish, sea monsters and dolphins. Decorated with seashells of different colours purchased in Holland (where they had been brought from the shores of the Indian Ocean), the pavilion was supposed to remind people of the sea, of the cool breeze off the waves. The original "grotesque" finish was replaced in the 1770s by stucco-work designed by the architect Antonio Rinaldi. The refurbished pavilion was styled "the Morning Hall".

In 1768 Catherine II decided to change the layout of the garden in keeping with the new vogue that had crossed the continent. She herself thought up landscape compositions, devised buildings of various styles and functions, and gradually the old, regular park was joined by natural-looking landscapes in the fashionable English style.

◀ *The Grotto pavilion. 1761, 1771*
Architects: Bartolomeo Francesco Rastrelli, Antonio Rinaldi

The Cameron Gallery
The Colonnade or Strolling Gallery

Catherine II dreamt of living in a house from the Ancient World and Cameron built her a whole complex of different structures including the Cold Bath and Agate Rooms, the Hanging Garden, the Ramp and the celebrated Cameron Gallery. The gallery, named in honour of its creator, rises above the Great Pond and seems to soar above the park.

Intended as a place for the Empress to stroll and enjoy philosophical conversations, the gallery had a long glazed hall at its cen-

The Cameron Gallery. Bust: Genius. 1795
St Petersburg. Cast by Edmonde Gastecloux:
copy of the original by Antonio Canova
Bronze (commissioned by Catherine II)

tre. On the open terraces around, between the columns, are bronze busts of ancient philosophers, scholars, poets, Roman emperors and military commanders.

Among the sculptures there is an interesting bronze bust of the "Russian Leonardo", Mikhailo Lomonosov, created by his friend Fedot Shubin.

Today it is hard to imagine the Catherine Park without the Cameron Gallery, so much has that building come to embody the character of the whole park ensemble. It is rare anywhere to find such a perfect combination of nature and architecture. The gallery altered the relatively level landscape of Tsarskoye Selo: before its construction the area seemed flat, but the installation of a tremendous flight of steps descending from the second storey straight into the garden created an impression of relief.

The steps divide at the top into two sweeping flights, while its piers serve as pedestals for two colossal bronze statues *Hercules* and *Flora* that were cast from ancient originals by the sculptor Fiodor Gordeyev and the founder Mozhalov.

From the gallery visitors reach the small Hanging Garden — an open area at second-storey level. The tops of the supporting vaults were covered in lead topped with a thick layer of earth

The Cameron Gallery. The facade on the side of the Flower Garden (Ladies'-in-Waiting Garden)

that made it possible to grow shrubs and trees here. Adjoining the Hanging Garden is the south facade of the Agate Rooms. The entrance to this pavilion takes the form of a rotunda-portico with columns and a small, shallow dome.

The Cold Bath or Agate Rooms occupies a central place in the complex of structures created by Cameron. The composition reflects above all the architect's fascination with Roman *thermae*, public baths, which he had spent more than twenty years studying. The external design, layout and interiors decorated with exquisite taste are veritably steeped in the spirit of Antiquity.

The architectural approach taken in the Agate Rooms is exceptional in its refined simplicity and precise proportions. The lower storey is faced with blocks of Pudost stone — roughly worked and porous, as if eaten away by wind and rain, which produces the illusion of a truly "ancient monument". It links the pavilion with the Cameron Gallery and gives integrity to the whole complex. The second storey, by contrast, is high and bright. Its walls are painted in a tender shade of yellow that sets off niches the colour of terracotta that contain stone statues and the tall rectangular "French" balconies with exquisite railings. Above Cameron placed round moulded bas-relief medallions containing mythological compositions. The facade is decorated with bronze statues and busts (copies of ancient originals) and also representations of the four elements by the French sculptor Lambert Sigisbert Adam.

The Agate Rooms (The Cold Bath). 1780–88
Architect: Charles Cameron

The Agate Rooms. The Large Hall

The rooms in the lower floor of the Cold Bath were intended for bathing, massage and relaxation. There was also a "hot bath" here — a warm room with heated water. The vaults, coving and walls of the frigidarium, a room containing a swimming-pool, were decorated by the sculptor Jacques-Dominique Rachette with exquisite medallions, sculptural friezes and multi-figure panels on classical subjects. Cameron's unsurpassed mastery as an interior decorator expressed itself with particular

The Agate Rooms
The Large Hall. Sculpture Cupid
Wagging His Finger. After 1757
Sculptor: Etienne Maurice Falconet
Autor's replica (?)

strength in the second storey. The decor of the Jasper and Agate Cabinets that flank the large central hall is just as rich as that of the palace state rooms and takes the form of a highly valuable "collection" of minerals from the Ural and Altai mountains. The variety of coloured stone facing the walls of the rooms have given the pavilion its second name.

The main hall of the Agate Rooms, intended for balls and concerts, was inspired by one of the rooms in Diocletian's baths. The matt gleam of the walls, lined with artificial marble of a tender peach colour, the grey-pink Olonets marble of the eight Corinthian columns, the white marble torcheres in the form of classical female figures supporting gilded lamps, and

jasper and porphyry vases set in niches create a noble colour scheme. This refined range of hues is complemented by doors veneered with mahogany and palisander and the multicoloured pattern of the parquet floor designed by Yury Velten. The vaults of the hall are decorated with stucco and paintings. There are numerous ornaments made of gilded bronze.

The Hanging Garden, raised on great piers, links the Agate Rooms to the Cameron Gallery and the second storey of the Catherine Palace. In turn both edifices are linked to the landscape park by the gently-sloping Ramp. A succession of mighty arches on Doric columns gradually descends to an alley of the park. This arcade, faced with limestone, is embellished with key-

The Ramp. 1787, 1826
Architects: Charles Cameron, Vasily Stasov

The Meadow by the Cameron Gallery
19th century. Watercolour by M. Martynov

stones decorated with masks of classical deities. The texture, colour, faultlessly struck proportions of the diminishing arcade, seeming to go down into the ground, masks of Mercury, Apollo, Neptune, Diana and other gods together produce an impression of profound antiquity. The spirit of Ancient Greece and Rome, the spirit of history itself, seems to hover above this corner of the park, recalling the eternity of existence and the fleeting nature of life. Originally the Ramp was adorned by bronze figures of the Greek muses. The muses and other statues from the Ramp were moved to Pavlovsk and, as early as Alexander I's reign, the architect Vasily Stasov filled the empty pedestals with

The Ramp. Mask on a keystone. 1787
Architect: Charles Cameron

iron vases in the form of ancient altars. These structures filled the garden with a natural classical simplicity and demonstrated the new possibilities made available by the aesthetic interaction of the strict forms of Classical architecture with a man-made picturesque landscape. Cameron's brilliant creation is removed from the water and raised high above the expanse of the lake, as if floating in the air, providing a panorama of the surroundings. From its colonnades there is a fine view of the Great Pond, known also as the Great Lake, on account of its size. The lake with its 16-hectare surface shapes the entire area around with fine vistas and large meadows sweeping down to the water. It has an irregular stretched shape oriented north-east to south-west. Three headlands, together with the man-made islands, act as if they are elements in some great stage decoration, revealing and concealing from sight the architectural monuments that unexpectedly meet the visitors' gaze.

The Cameron Gallery

*Sculpture **Hercules** by the steps
of the Cameron Gallery. 1785
Sculptor: Fiodor Gordeyev, from
an ancient original*

The Great Lake. The Hall on the Island. Sculpture: **The Discus-Thrower**
*1848. The galvanoplastic workshop of J. Hamburger, from
the Ancient Greek original by Myron*

Artificial islands and a meandering shoreline made the Great Pond resemble a real lake. On the island in the middle of the lake stands the Concert Hall that in the eighteenth century was known very simply as "the Hall on the Island". Built by Rastrelli in 1750, the pavilion was converted to the Classical style in 1794 by Giacomo Quarenghi and reworked again in 1817–19 by Vasily Stasov and Piotr Neyelov.

The Hall on the Island was used for musical soirees and dances during festivities. Besides the usual run of court occasions, several times in the second half of the eighteenth century Tsarskoye Selo was the scene for tremendous illuminations. Boat trips on the lake were a fairly common amusement for Catherine the Great and her court. Such events were usually accompanied by music: choir singing at the Admiralty, wind instruments at other places.

The Admiralty, built by Vasily Neyelov in 1777 in mock Gothic style, is made up of several buildings: a boathouse, two aviary wings and a house for the boatsmen. Black and white swans, peafowl, pheasants and ducks were kept in the aviaries. Boats were kept downstairs in the boathouse, while above there was the Dutch Hall decorated with tinted English engravings of parks. A dam was constructed next to the Admiralty with an adjoining landing-stage.

The Great Lake. View of the Chesme Column and Turkish Bath

The Chesme Column seems to emerge directly from the smooth waters of the Great Pond. It commemorates Russian naval success in the Russo-Turkish War of 1768–74 and was constructed between 1768 and 1776 to a design by Antonio Rinaldi. The Olonets marble monument has a base of grey Serdobol granite. The rostral column is crowned by a bronze eagle with wings outspread tearing apart a Turkish crescent. There are bas-reliefs of sea battles on three sides of the base.

The Chesme Column features in the poetry of Pushkin. It commemorates a brilliant victory gained in the Aegan in the year 1770, when seventeen ships of the Russian navy destroyed a much larger enemy force.

The wars against Turkey were a key feature of Russian foreign policy in the second half of the eighteenth century. Catherine II twice made war on the Ottoman Empire. In the course of those conflicts Russia conquered the Crimea and northern shores of the Black Sea. Every success in this conflict was marked by an edifice of some kind at Tsarskoye Selo.

Past victories over Turkey are also recalled by the Turkish Bath constructed by Ippolito Monighetti in the mid-nineteenth century in the manner of a Turkish mosque.

The Marble (or Palladian) Bridge completes the panorama of the Great Pond. Harmonious proportions and an inspired selection of different coloured marble in combination with a grey granite base have made this structure one of the finest adornments of the Catherine Park.

◀ *The Chesme Column. 1776. Architect: Antonio Rinaldi*

The Turkish Bath. 1852. Architect: Ippolito Monighetti

*The Marble (Palladian) Bridge
1777. Architect: Vasily Neyelov* ▶

A characteristic feature of English-style parks — the succession of different landscapes — is clearly in evidence in the Catherine Park. A stroll around the lake brings ever-changing vistas including a whole variety of buildings, some of which are quite surprising.

The pyramid constructed in 1770–73 by Vasily Neyelov is a copy of the tomb of one of the Roman caesars. It is made of brick and faced with dark granite. Here, on the banks of a channel running around the overgrown islets known as the Swan Islands,

Catherine II buried her favourite dogs. (Before the war one could find marble tombstones engraved with humorous verses devoted to these pets.)

Between 1778 and 1782 the Gothic Gates were erected in this part of the park. The cast-iron gates were produced in the distant Urals city of Yekaterinburg to the design of the architect Yury Velten and are testimony to the high level of development that Russian industry had attained by the 1770s. The gates are twelve metres high and almost seven metres wide.

The Pyramid. 1773, 1783. Architects: Vasily Neyelov, Charles Cameron

◀ *The Gothic Gates. 1778–82. Architect: Yury Velten*

The Tower Ruin. 1773. Architect: Yury Velten

The Tower Ruin was designed by Yury Velten as a belvedere, a high vantage-point from which to enjoy views of the landscape park. It was constructed in the year 1771–73 with deliberate cracks and dents in its walls making it resemble a batterd mediaeval castle. It is topped by an apparently time-ravaged pavilion on a rectangular platform that can be reached by asending an earth mound imitating a castle rampart. The inscription carved on the stone in the centre of the brick arch reads "In memory of the war declared on Russia by the Turks, this stone was set in place in 1768."

The Orlov Gate was constructed in 1777–82 at the edge of the park where it gives onto the road to Gatchina. It was designed by Antonio Rinaldi in the form of a triumphal arch with a single passageway. The gate's austere lines are emphasized by the rich framing. The inscription in the frieze is a line taken from a letter written in verse by the poet Vasily Maikov and reveals the significance of the edifice — "Moscow has been delivered from misfortune by Orlov". It commemorates Count Grigory Orlov's successful struggle against an epidemic of plague in the old capital in 1771. (Orlov was the first of the Catherine II's favourites.) The gate is built of brick and faced with Olonets and Siberian marble of different colours. The wrought-iron leaves of the gate have an austere design enlivened by attached bronze elements. They were produced from drawings by Quarenghi at the Sestroretsk Arms Factory in 1787.

The Gatchina (Orlov) Gate. 1777–82
Architect: Antonio Rinaldi ▶

With its small red towers pierced by narrow lancet arches and slit windows, the Red or Turkish Cascade, constructed by Vasily Neyelov in the 1770s near the Tower Ruin, is one more architectural variation on the theme of the Russo-Turkish Wars. The narrow deep-set embrasures make the cascade look like a fortification of some kind.

The landscape area of the park, from the Orlov Gate to the Great Pond, was created in the 1770s by the architect Vasily Neyelov and the master gardeners Joseph Bush and T. Il-yin. Their efforts produced artificial hills, bridges and dams. A host of weir-cascades were produced by the hydraulic engineer I. Gerard as a decorative feature. One of the dams situated on the Upper Ponds is decorated with a hill of tufa and limestone. Its base contains a grotto with water spurting through a small opening. In old descriptions of the Catherine Park, the hill of natural rock is called the "mossy cliff".

The Wild Hill weir-bridge. 1770s. Engineer: I. Gerard

◀ *The Red (Turkish) Cascade. 1770s. Architect: Vasily Neyelov*

The Granite (Rusca) Terrace. 1809
Architect: Luigi Rusca

The Granite Terrace created in 1809 to plans by Luigi Rusca is a sort of viewing platform of rose-coloured granite set off by grey columns. An elegant balustrade and flights of steps at the edges bring out the shape of the hill on which the terrace lies. It is people by figures from mythology created by the galvanoplastic method in the workshop of J. Hamburger and installed here in 1860. (This method, invented in the nineteenth century, used electrolysis in conjunction with a mould to produce fine castings.)

The bronze figure of a young girl in classical dress, frozen in sadness over a broken pitcher, presents itself to us as a symbol of sorrow, unfulfilled hopes and poetic dreams. A granite rock near the Great Lake serves as a pedestal for the bronze sculpture.

A stream of clear water flows from the broken vessel. A natural underground spring was converted into a fountain by the engineer Augustin Bethencourt in 1810. The sculpture, by Pavel Sokolov, was added in 1816 on the instructions of Alexander I. The touching sight of the "girl with the pitcher" has inspired many poets. Pushkin called her simply "the Tsarskoye Selo statue" and the name has stuck.

*The **Milkmaid Fountain** or The Girl with a Pitcher. 1816. Sculptor: Pavel Sokolov* ▶

The Concert Hall, created by Giacomo Quarenghi in 1786 in an austere Classical style as "a hall for music and a temple dedicated to the goddess Ceres", might be said to be filled with Antiquity. The hall was intended for summer concerts. It is located on an island and almost hidden among the trees which creates the elegiac atmosphere typical of pavilions in a landscape park that seem to appear by chance on the winding path. The Concert Hall resembles a miniature Pantheon, another feature of many an "English park" (a notable example can be found in the garden of Chiswick House in London). The surfaces of the walls are pierced by tall rectangular windows without architraves. It is as if an open rotunda with ten columns and a shallow dome has been cut into the body of the building.

Close to the Concert Hall is the small Ruin Kitchen, also designed by Quarenghi. It looks like a shanty from the outside and was used for reheating food during concerts and balls. Interestingly, genuine elements from ancient buildings have been incorporated into the walls of the Ruin Kitchen.

The Ruin Kitchen. 1786. Architect: Giacomo Quarenghi; sculptor: Concesio Albani

◄ *The Concert Hall. 1786. Architect: Giacomo Quarenghi*

The Great Caprice. *From the album* **Twelve Views of Tsarskoye Selo.** *1820. Lithograph from a watercolour by Valerian Langer*

The Evening Hall is a single-storey pavilion intended for concerts, musical soirees and balls. The hall took almost fifteen years to build — from 1796 to 1809. It was begun to a design by Piotr Neyelov and completed by Luigi Rusca. The main facade is adorned by a portico with four Ionic columns. An exquisite airiness is the hallmark of the decoration. The facade and the decorative painting inside the building were restored in 1990.

In the 1780s a monument in the form of a flaming urn on a tall rectangular pedestal faced with a variety of marble was set up on a meadow close to the Concert Hall. This sentimental creation appeared at the behest of Cathe-rine II and was styled "the monument for services". Later it was dedicated to Alexander Lanskoi, a favourite of the Empress who died young. Catherine was genuinely attached to this elegant, handsome young man who literally infected her with a passion for collecting cameos. The unexpected death from scarlet fever of the 26-year-old general, gentleman-in-waiting and colonel-in-chief of the Cuirassiers Regiment shook the Empress very deeply. After his death a bronze plaque was added to the pedestal bearing Lanskoi's coat of arms and enlarged relief depictions of both sides of the medal struck in his memory. The monument was restored in 1977.

Monument to Lanskoi. 1780s
Architect: Antonio Rinaldi ▶

The creation in the 1770s of the Great and Little Caprices — features in the form of man-made hills pierced by arches — is evidence that Catherine the Great was strongly influenced by the prevailing vogue for all things Oriental. The tall arch of the Great Caprice spans the road that separates the Catherine and Alexander Parks. On top of it stands a belvedere with a curving painted roof in imitation Chinese style. Built by Vasily Neyelov and Gerard, the Great Caprice was the main entrance to the parks of Tsarskoye Selo in Catherine's time. Paths running over the crest of the hills made it possible

The Great Caprice. 1770–74
Architect: Vasily Neyelov;
engineer: I. Gerard. 1780s
Architect: Giacomo Quarenghi

The Great Caprice. *From the album* Twelve Views of Tsarskoye Selo. *1820. Lithograph from a watercolour by Valerian Langer*

The Chinese or Creaking Summerhouse. 1778–86. Architect: Yury Velten

to walk from one part of the park to the other without crossing the carriageway. The top provides a fine view of the palace and parks.

The Creaking Summer-House, another pavilion in imitation Chinese style, was created between 1778 and 1786 by the architect Yury Velten. The weathervane on the roof of the building produces a grating noise when turned by the wind and that gave rise to the name. The roof resting on twelve columns with its fancifully curved edges and brightly painted dragons on the corners, the elaborately shaped windows and doors, the railing of the terrace and the flight of steps descending like a fan to the water are all indications that the architect was absorbed with the picturesque quaintness of Chinoiserie in garden pavilions. This exotic architecture of small forms came to Russia in the late 1760s.

The Chinese Village. 1780s, 1817–22. Architects: Charles Cameron, Vasily Stasov

The idea of creating a Chinese Village dates from the first half of the 1770s. Antonio Rinaldi and Vasily Neyelov worked on the project. They devised a village consisting of a small street lined with little Chinese houses, four on each side, and a octagonal square containing a two-tier pagoda-observatory in the centre. The design of the observatory was borrowed from an engraving of a Chinese pagoda published by the East India Company in its seventeenth-century *Description of the Chinese Empire*. It was proposed to mark the entrance to the village with a gate like a Chinese *pai-loo* covered with a pitched roof. Cameron began to realise the project in the 1780s, but managed to complete only ten buildings of the planned eighteen.

In 1817–22 Vasily Stasov continued the work. He connected the houses in pairs and, changing their internal layout made them suitable as dwellings. In the nineteenth century the Chinese Village was used as official housing for courtiers.

The noted historian Nikolai Karamzin lived in one of the houses in the 1820s. Despite repeated reconstructions the buildings have retained their Chinese flavour. The facades are decorated with colourful painting in an Oriental style, but the real attraction of the houses is their multicoloured painted roofs, decorated with dragons, dolphins, umbrellas and other whimsical "Chinese" elements. Nowadays the buildings are used as housing and guest accommodation.

◀ *The Chinese Village*

The Private Garden by the Zubov Wing
The pergola. 1866. Architect: A. Vidov

Monuments to military glory are a distinctive feature of the Tsarskoye Selo parks. The Kagul, or Rumiantsev, Obelisk was erected to mark the victory gained by forces commanded by Count Piotr Rumiantsev over the Turks in a battle fought on the River Kagul in Moldavia on 1 August (21 July) 1770. Both obelisk and pedestal are made of blue marble with white veins.

The pedestal rises from a granite platform surrounded by granite pillars. The Kagul Obelisk, like the two rostral columns in the park, the smaller Morea and larger Chesme Column, dedicated to Russian naval victories, was for many contemporaries above all a place of remembrance marking what were in their time great and historic events.

In 1855 part of the park in front of the southern, Zubov wing of the Catherine Palace was converted into the Private Garden that was reserved for the family of Emperor Alexander II and his close entourage.

Ten years later a fountain designed by the architect Vidov was installed in the garden. The large octagonal basin, bowl and small vases placed around the edge of the basin were produced from white Carrara marble at the Peterhof Lapidary Works.

Here too an open veranda or pergola in the Italian style was created. The gallery of the pergola is formed by two rows of classical columns made of light grey sandstone. Both fountain basin and pergola are decorated with round marble vases.

The Kagul Obelisk. 1772. Architect: Antonio Rinaldi ▶

The Alexander Palace and Park

The central Golden Gate to the grand courtyard of the Catherine Palace. 1752–56
Produced at the Sestroretsk Arms Factory to a design by Bartolomeo Francesco Rastrelli

*H*istorically the Alexander (New) Garden consisted of two parts. The "regular" area with a precise geometrical layout was created in the middle of the eighteenth century. It is enclosed on all sides by the Krestovy Canal. Two intersecting main alleys divide this part of the park into four sections, each of which has its own centre for the amusement of visitors. The more distant landscape park was laid out in the 1820s in place of the palace menagerie (an enclosed area of woodland for hunting).

The architectural structures in the Alexander Park were created in the second half of the eighteenth century and the first half of the nineteenth to designs by Vasily Neyelov, Charles Cameron and Adam Menelaws. Cameron, in particular, was responsible for the Large Chinese Bridge with vases at the entrance to the Alexander Park, a second granite bridge with sculptures of winged dragons parallel to it at the end of the Triple Lime Alley and two Small Chinese Bridges.

 *The Large Chinese Bridge. 1786. Architect: Charles Cameron*

◀ *The Small Chinese Bridges. 1787. Architect: Charles Cameron*

The Dragon Bridge. 1786. Architect: Charles Cameron; sculptor: P. Schwartz

The Arsenal. 1819–34
Architects: Adam Menelaws, Konstantin Thon

In contrast to the Catherine Park, all the architectural edifices in the Alexander Park appeared almost simultaneously, with one and the same Neo-Gothic style, and were the work of the one architect, Adam Menelaws (a Scottish master mason turned architect who had come to Russia in 1784). The fashion for "Gothic" pavilions was encouraged by Nicholas I. The knightly dress and customs of the Middle Ages held a great attraction for the Emperor and on his initiative tournaments and masquerades were held in the park.

In 1819 Menelaws began constructing the Arsenal on the site of the Monbijou hunting-lodge. After the architect's death the work was completed by Konstantin Thon, who gave the building the look of a Gothic castle, obviously in imitation of such British prototypes as the belvedere on Shrub's Hill, Windsor. In 1834 Nicholas I's collection of arms and armour was installed here (in 1885 it was transferred to the Hermitage). The Arsenal building is still awaiting restoration.

In 1828, in the same part of the park, Menelaws constructed another edifice of considerable size and interesting conception. The Chapelle, as it is known, looks like the ruins of a Gothic church. It occupies a site that until 1825 belonged a pavilion on the southern bastion of the Menagerie and is regarded as a masterpiece of "ruin architecture". Its towers, half-collapsed walls, columns and lancet stained-glass windows exude an enchanting air of great age. Inside the Chapelle stood a statue of the Saviour by the German sculptor Johann Heinrich von Dannecker.

The Chapelle. 1828. Architect: Adam Menelaws ▶

The Llama Pavilion. 1823. Architect: Adam Menelaws

In 1823 Menelaws built a pavilion in the Alexander Park to house the llamas that had been brought from South America. Besides stables and a small covered exercise area, the complex also included accommodation for the keeper, a fodder store and a sixteen-metre-high tower containing a small room for resting.

The three-tier tower with a crenellated parapet adjoined the two-storey building. In 1860 the architect Ippolito Monighetti adapted part of the building for use as a photographic studio and laboratory. The considerable damage caused here during the war has still not been rectified.

Architecture of this sort was a tribute to the romanticism and fascination with history that seized Russian society after the "Patriotic War" of 1812.

The mock Gothic style made use of mediaeval attributes (arches, towers, vaults) for purely decorative purposes. Ruin pavilions transformed the surrounding landscape. The half-light of densely overgrown alleys, tall trees, winding paths and different little bridges endow the park with a mysterious, romantic character.

The Alexander Park is one of the most romantic landscape parks in Russia. On its northern side, the Alexander Palace was erected in the late eighteenth century on the bank of a man-made pond.

The Alexander Park

The Alexander Palace. 1792–96
Architect: Giacomo Quarenghi

By 1796 Giacomo Quarenghi had finished construction of the Alexander Palace, intended as a residence for Catherine II's eldest grandson, the future Alexander I. The new building fitted neatly into the surrounding park. The two-storey building with twin side-wings and a magnificent Corinthian colonnade was notable for its harmonious proportions. The colonnade linked the side-wings of the palace and connected it with the space of the park.

The state rooms inside the palace were arranged in an enfilade and consisted of several apartments divided by arches. Despite the exquisite finishing of both state rooms and private quarters, when he had become emperor, Alexander I preferred to use the Catherine Palace, giving the newer residence over to his younger brother Nicholas. When Nicholas came to the throne, he wanted to turn the Alexander Palace into an imperial summer residence. From 1831 onwards he and his family spent the greater part of the summer months here. At that time alterations were made to many of the state and private rooms. Later Nicholas I's grandson, the future Alexander III, moved into the palace. His apartments were located in the right-hand wing of the building.

The most significant period in the history of the Alexander Palace, however, came in the reign of Emperor Nicholas II who was born in Tsarskoye Selo and took up permanent residence in the Alexander Palace in 1905.

The Alexander Palace. The left wing with the personal apartments of the last Russian emperor ▶

For Nicholas and his family the palace became a cosy "nest" associated with happy events. After the February Revolution in 1917 and Nicholas's abdication, it was where the ex-Tsar and his family were kept until they were moved to Siberia. Their first destination was Tobolsk. From there they were taken to Yekaterinburg where they met their untimely end.

Later a museum was opened in the Alexander Palace, devoted to the "daily life of the House of Romanov". Despite the considerable damage inflicted on the palace during the occupation, its internal decor survived. At present there is a display about Nicholas II and his family in the restored part of the palace.

Portrait of Emperor Alexander I. *1815*
Watercolour by Jean-Baptiste Isabey

The State (New, Large) Study of Nicholas II
1906. Architect: Robert Melzer

he personal apartments of the last Russian emperor were located in the left wing of the palace. A long corridor separated the apartments into two parts: Alexandra Fiodorovna's suite and Nicholas II's. The Large State (New) Study completed a succession of the Emperor's personal rooms (Working Study, Reception Room and Dining-Room) on the right side of the corridor. The State Study was created by the brothers Robert and Friedrich Melzer in 1903 in the *Moderne* style, a Russian variant of the Art Nouveau. The mahogany panelling, two fireplaces, the gallery with columns, and the brass-bound ceiling panels survived and were restored in 1947–51. The wall decoration and furnishings recreated from measurements and pictorial records together with items of applied art, paintings and photographs that were evacuated enable us to see the study as it was in the time of its last owner. The New Study was used for sessions of the Council of Ministers. It also contained a billiard table on which the Tsar liked to play with his friends.

The Marble (State) Study of Nicholas II
Detail of the interior ▶

The exhibition Reminiscences
in the Alexander Palace

The Emperor and Empress lived their happy family life in this palace, hidden from prying eyes. This was a separate magical world to which only a limited number of people were admitted. For many years the palace remained their private home. The Empress took charge of the decoration and under her guidance the apartments took on the appearance of a cosy English house. Following Alexandra Fiodorovna's wishes, Richard Melzer decorated the living apartments in the *Moderne* style. The left part of the enfilade contained the Empress's Bed Chamber, Lilac Study and Palisander Draw-

ing-Room, the right part Nicholas's working and official rooms. The splendid decoration of these rooms, damaged but not ruined during the war, was destroyed in the post-war reconstruction of the palace as being of little artistic value and not worthy of attention.

A lift and stairs led to the children's rooms on the upper floor. The rooms of the couple's four daughters were simply and practically furnished: they slept on special camp-beds, almost without pillows, under thin blankets. The same simplicity marked the bedroom and playroom of Tsesarevich Alexei, the heir to the throne. The

Mosaic icon of St Alexandra
1894. St Petersburg

as nurses and assisted in a military hospital.

The centre of the happy family was its youngest member, Tsarevich Alexei, a bright, attractive child, afflicted with haemophilia. His illness was the family's personal secret, one that they carefully sought to keep from the world.

Alexandra Fiodorovna wholeheartedly accepted the Orthodox faith before her marriage to Nicholas II in 1894. The long-awaited heir's illness drained his mother's spiritual strength and constantly shaped her thoughts and actions. There were icons everywhere in the residential part of the palace, some 700 in the bedroom alone. Religious faith was the Empress's only succour, prayer her only comfort in the face of a trying fate.

◄ *Mosaic icon of St Nicholas the Miracle-Worker. Late 19th century. St Petersburg*

children took a cold bath in the mornings. They were clothed economically with dresses and shoes being handed down from one to another. The whole family came together for meals in the small Reception Room created by Melzer in 1896–98. The furniture was plain and comfortable; table and shelves were kept in perfect order. But they were more fond of gathering in the Empress's cosy Palisander Room. The four daughters — Olga, Tatiana, Maria and Anastasia — were great friends despite the differences in their characters. Olga was most like her father. Tatiana, the slimmest and most elegant of the sisters, resembled the Empress. Maria, the third daughter, stood out for her generous, happy disposition, while Anastasia, the youngest, amused people with her pranks. The girls were taught to keep house and to perform certain public duties. During the First World War the Empress and her older daughters trained

Marie Antoinette and her Children
Tapestry from a painting by Elisabeth Vigée-Lebrun. 1900s. France

Princess Alix Victoria Helena Louise Beatrice of Hesse-Darmstadt, known from childhood simply as Alix, was a typical Victorian in character. The granddaughter of the great British Queen, brought up and educated in England, she was more like an English woman than a German. To the end of her days she spoke with an English accent, loved punctuality and strict order. It was this strikingly attractive woman, elegantly dressed, who created the cosy world in which the recluses of Tsarskoye Selo lived.

The Empress's apartments began with the Maple Drawing-Room. A raised gallery was created in the room that communicated with

Nicholas's apartments through the gallery in the adjoining State Study. Both the study and the drawing-room were created in 1906 to Robert Melzer's designs in place of Quarenghi's Concert Hall. The space was divided up into cosy corners in which the whole family gathered in the evenings. The balconies in the corners were adorned with palms and a twining vine.

It was in the Lilac Study that the Empress spent much of her time. Here she met friends, drank tea in the evening, read out loud and let the children play. There was an upright piano, music, drawing and handicraft articles and children's board games. The rooms contained blossoming and decorative pot-plants. Lilac, roses, lilies of the valley and other flowers stood on a table by the window. The Empress disliked chandeliers and only table-lights and shaded wall-lights lit her rooms in the evening.

◀ *A. Bodarevsky.* **Portrait of Empress Alexandra Fiodorovna.** *1907*

The Alexander Palace. The Corner Drawing-Room of Empress Alexandra Fiodorovna. 1796. Architect: Giacomo Quarenghi

The Corner Drawing-Room was created by Quarenghi in 1796 and belonged to the suite of state rooms in his palace. The white artificial marble walls were originally embellished with five large mirrors. In Alexandra Fiodorovna's time the marble finish was retained. In the 1900s the interior was adorned by items produced at the Svirsky and Melzer factories, two concert grand pianos and a harmonium, a host of portraits, busts and miniatures, and also a tapestry of Marie Antoinette and her children that was a gift from President Loubet of France.

In the Corner Drawing-Room the Empress received ministers, foreign ambassadors and deputations. Concerts were arranged here in which members of the imperial family participated. The famous Russian singer Feodor Chaliapin performed here. Several sessions of the Imperial Historical Society were held here. The decor, damaged during the war, has been restored.

Today this room forms part of the display entitled "Reminiscences in the Alexander Palace" that opened in August 1997.

This display extends through a number of rooms belonging to the family apartments that were damaged in the Second World War and lost their appearance during the postwar years.

In 1909 work began on the construction of the Fiodorovsky Cathedral on grounds separated off from the Alexander Park. Soon nearby a whole town was constructed to plans by the architects Pokrovsky, Krichinsky and Maximov. The cathedral and some buildings of the Fiodorovsky Town were designed in the style of Old Russian architecture of the sixteenth and seventeenth centuries, in keeping with efforts to revive a distinctively national style in architecture, using the forms of the time before Peter I. The imperial family often visited the cathedral and a special prayer chapel was constructed in the crypt for Alexandra Fiodorovna.

Work on the Fiodorovsky Town was interrupted in 1917. Services have now resumed in the restored cathedral.

The Fiodorovsky Cathedral ▶
1909–12. Architects: Vladimir Pokrovsky and Alexander Pomerantsev; artist: N. Yemelyanov; mosaicist: Vladimir Frolov

Tower of the Fiodorovsky Town
1913–16. Architect: Stepan Krichinsky;
artist: N. Pashkov; ceramist: Piotr Vaulin

Panorama of the Fiodorovsky Town

The Egyptian Gate — the entrance to Tsarskoye Selo on the road from St Petersburg — was built in 1827–30 to the design of the architect Adam Menelaws on the site of the barrier that restricted entry to the town. Blocks in the form of truncated pyramids served as guardhouses. Their outer walls are made of brick and faced with cast-iron panels bearing relief depictions of scenes from the mythology and daily life of the Ancient Egyptians. The cornices are decorated with images of sun-discs, snakes' heads and scarab beetles that were sacred in the Egyptian culture. Mysterious hieroglyphic messages from long-dead pharaohs complement the reliefs. The models for these castings were produced in clay by Vasily De-

The Egyptian Gate. Scenes from Ancient Egyptian life

◄ *The Egyptian Gate. Herm obelisk with the head of a pharaoh. 1830 Architect: Adama Menelaws*

muth-Malinovsky from drawings by the artist Dodonov. The Russians were repeating authentic Egyptian originals reproduced in a multi-volume work published in Paris early in the nineteenth century. Their creations are evidence of the appearance of new prototypes in nineteenth century art.

By the walls of the guardhouses there are majestic cast-iron herms with the heads of pharaohs. Herms of the same kind, but double-sided serve as pillars for the gates. The grille of fine rods in the form of lotus stems topped with flowers were, like the iron reliefs, cast at the Alexandrovsky Foundry in St Petersburg. The Ancient Egyptians extend their welcome, as it were, to all those who come to Tsarskoye Selo in search of its beauty.

The Egyptian Gate. 1830 Architect: Adam Menelaws ▶

*The Egyptian Gate. Image of Maat,
the goddess of truth and
patroness of justice*

Царское Село. Дворцы и парки

Альбом (на английском языке)

Издательство «Альфа-Колор», Санкт-Петербург
Тел./факс (812) 326-8384 E-mail: alfac@mail.wplus.net